D0538782

Surviving Earthquakes

Michael Burgan

Raintree

Chicago, Illinois

www.heinemannraintree.com
Visit our website to find out more information about Heinemann-Raintree books.

To order:
☎ Phone 888-454-2279
🖥 Visit www.heinemannraintree.com
to browse our catalog and order online.

Edited by Louise Galpine and Laura Knowles
Designed by Victoria Allen
Original illustrations © Capstone Global Library Limited 2011
Illustrated by HLSTUDIOS
Picture research by Ruth Blair

Originated by Capstone Global Library Limited
Printed and bound in China by CTPS

15 14 13 12 11
10 9 8 7 6 5 4 3 2 1

Library of Congress Cataloging-in-Publication Data
Burgan, Michael.
  Surviving earthquakes / Michael Burgan.—1st ed.
    p. cm.—(Children's true stories: natural disasters)
  Includes bibliographical references and index.
  ISBN 978-1-4109-4090-2 (hc)—ISBN 978-1-4109-4097-1 (pb) 1. Earthquakes—History—Juvenile literature. 2. Disaster victims—Psychological aspects—Juvenile literature. I. Title.
  HV599.B87 2012
  363.34'950922—dc22   2010036178

4732 8819 10/11

Acknowledgments
We would like to thank the following for permission to reproduce photographs: © Corbis p. 7; Corbis pp. 5 (TRACEY NEARMY/epa), **8** (© Bettmann), **9** (© Bettmann), **11** (© Grant Smith), **13** (© Bettmann), **14** (© Bettmann), **19** (© CHINA DAILY/Reuters), **21** (© HO/Reuters), **25** (© MCSN Aaron Shelley/U.S. Navy/Handout/Navy Visual News Service (NVNS)); Getty Images pp. **15** (Keystone), **22** (AFP), **23** (Digital Vision), **27** (SAM YEH/AFP); Library of Congress pp. **10**; PA Photos pp. **18** (© LANDOV), **24** (© J Pat Carter/AP); © USGS p. **17**.

Cover photograph of survivors of Haiti's earthquake walking along a dump near downtown Port-au-Prince, February 9, 2010, reproduced with permission of Corbis/© Ivan Alvarado/Reuters.

Quotations on pages 6, 8, and 9 are from DeWitt C. Baldwin, "Memories of the San Francisco Earthquake and Fire" as related to Ana Maria P. de Jesus, September 19, 1988, The Virtual Museum of the City of San Francisco, www.sfmuseum.net. Quotations on pages 13, 14, and 15 are from Joshua Hammer, *Yokohama Burning* (New York: Free Press, 2006). Quotation on page 17 is from Andrew H. Malcolm, "Chinese Disclose That 1976 Quake Was Deadliest in Four Centuries," *New York Times*, June 1977. Quotations on pages 18 and 19 are from Eugene Tang and William Bi, "Tangshan Survivor Drives 1,200 Miles to Give China Quake Relief," Bloomberg.com, May 16, 2008. Quotations on pages 23 and 24 are from Haroon Siddique, "Girl Found Alive 15 Days After Haiti Quake," *The Guardian*, January 28, 2010.

We would like to thank Daniel Block for his invaluable help in the preparation of this book.

Every effort has been made to contact copyright holders of material reproduced in this book. Any omissions will be rectified in subsequent printings if notice is given to the publisher.

Disclaimer
All the Internet addresses (URLs) given in this book were valid at the time of going to press. However, due to the dynamic nature of the Internet, some addresses may have changed, or sites may have changed or ceased to exist since publication. While the author and publisher regret any inconvenience this may cause readers, no responsibility for any such changes can be accepted by either the author or the publisher.

Contents

DAILY LIFE
Read here to learn about what life was like for the children in these stories, and the impact the disaster had at home and school.

NUMBER CRUNCHING
Find out here the details about natural disasters and the damage they cause.

Survivors' lives
Read these boxes to find out what happened to the children in this book when they grew up.

HELPING HAND
Find out how people and organizations have helped to save lives.

On the scene
Read eyewitness accounts of the natural disasters in the survivors' own words.

Some words are printed in bold, **like this**. You can find out what they mean by looking in the glossary on page 30.

Introduction

It can happen at any moment. The ground rumbles and buildings shake. It's an earthquake! Earthquakes can be deadly events, but many people survive them. In this book you will read about children who experienced some of the worst earthquakes ever—and lived to tell the tale.

How do earthquakes happen?

Earth's surface is made up of giant, slow-moving slabs of rock called **tectonic plates**. Earthquakes can result when the two plates slide or push against each other. Most small earthquakes do not cause much damage. But strong earthquakes can topple or damage buildings, sometimes killing or injuring people trapped inside.

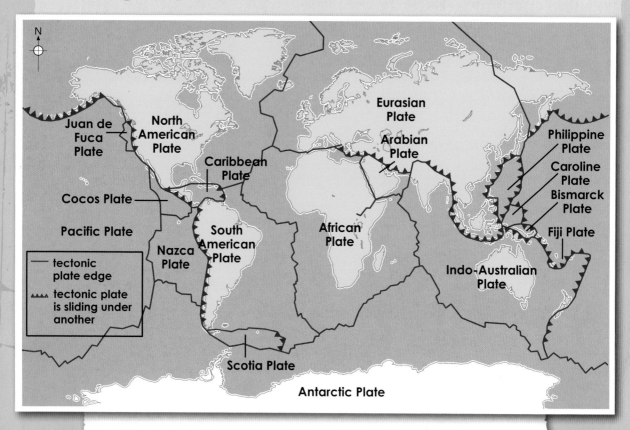

N

Juan de Fuca Plate

North American Plate

Caribbean Plate

Cocos Plate

Pacific Plate

Nazca Plate

South American Plate

African Plate

Eurasian Plate

Arabian Plate

Philippine Plate

Caroline Plate

Bismarck Plate

Fiji Plate

Indo-Australian Plate

Scotia Plate

Antarctic Plate

— tectonic plate edge

▴▴▴ tectonic plate is sliding under another

This map shows Earth's tectonic plates. Earthquakes usually occur where tectonic plates meet and cracks appear in Earth's surface. These areas are called **faults**.

A path of destruction

Earthquakes can also create **landslides**, which send rocks and earth tumbling down mountains and hillsides. Some earthquakes even create giant waves of water called **tsunamis**. The movement of the plates below the ocean stirs the wave. It moves quickly through deep water, gathering energy. When the tsunami hits shallow coastal areas, it is filled with destructive power.

On February 22, 2011 an earthquake destroyed much of the city of Christchurch, New Zealand. Rescue workers from around the world came to help find survivors.

San Francisco, California: 1906

DeWitt Baldwin rose before sunrise on April 18, 1906. The eight-year-old wanted to practice playing the piano before leaving for school. Suddenly, he felt the earth shake. As he later said, "Furniture moved at the violence of the shock."

Across San Francisco, California, people felt this first jolt from a powerful earthquake. Paved roads rippled like waves, and buildings began to collapse. The weight of crashing brick, stone, and wood killed some people instantly. Others were trapped in the **rubble**.

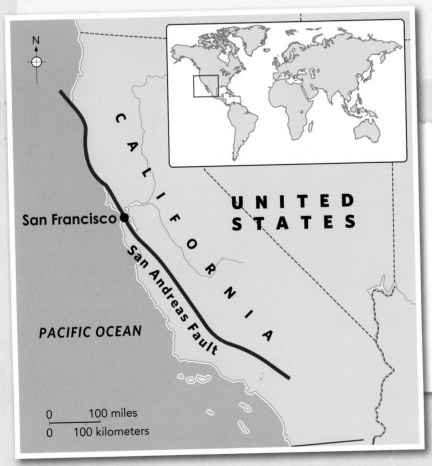

At around 1,300 kilometers (800 miles) long, the San Andreas Fault is the longest in California. Earthquakes along this **fault** have been some of the most destructive in U.S. history.

A second shake

In the Baldwin home, the damage was not so bad. The family got dressed and sat down for breakfast. Then a second **tremor** rattled the house. The true destruction of the earthquake was about to begin.

It is thought that more than 28,000 buildings were destroyed by the San Francisco earthquake and the fires that followed.

Claire Giannini's life

Claire Giannini (1904–1997) was just a toddler when the earthquake damaged her family's home. The fires then threatened to destroy her father's bank in San Francisco. Mr. Giannini ran his business in the street while the city was rebuilt, earning him great respect.

Years later Claire took over her father's bank, later known as Bank of America. She was one of the first women to play a major role in U.S. banking.

City in flames

Fires spread across San Francisco. The earthquake broke pipes carrying **natural gas**, and the smallest sparks set the gas on fire. DeWitt went outside. He remembered, "I came across a large crowd watching a huge department store ablaze. I observed how the firemen desperately attempted to bring the fire under control."

Fueling more fires

Firefighters struggled across the city. The earthquake damaged many of the water pipes they usually used to put out the flames. To slow the fire, the army began blowing up buildings. The plan was to remove the fuel the fires needed to grow. But some of the explosions simply caused new fires. Strong winds then spread the flames even more.

More than 50 separate fires broke out after the earthquake, including the ones accidentally started by the army.

This photograph shows the Winchester Hotel on fire. It was one of tens of thousands of buildings destroyed by the earthquake and fires.

On the scene

Toward the end of his life, DeWitt Baldwin described his thoughts as a child during the 1906 San Francisco earthquake: "The seriousness of the fire and all that it meant was gradually flooding my mind. My mind was then filled with genuine concern for others. . . . I began to realize as never before the importance of food, shelter, and protection."

9

Helping the homeless

The next day, the fires finally died down. They had missed the Baldwins' street, but other families were not so lucky. Their houses were destroyed, and they had to live in tents. About 225,000 people became **refugees**, left homeless by the earthquake. More than 3,000 people were killed.

Rebuilding the damage

San Francisco's leaders quickly began building new public buildings and office buildings. Houses soon followed. Within a few years, most signs of the damage were gone. Today, San Francisco is a bustling city of more than 800,000 people.

Thousands of tents were set up in city parks to provide shelter for people made homeless by the earthquake.

Danger remains

The threat of earthquakes remains for the people of San Francisco. The city sits along the San Andreas Fault (see map on page 6). This fault underneath California is the boundary between two major plates. It is around 800 miles (1,300 kilometers) long. Today, new buildings are built to stand up to earthquakes, but no building is completely safe. Despite the risk, people choose to live in San Francisco, even though they know another killer earthquake could strike at any moment.

Another major earthquake hit the San Francisco area in October 1989, damaging buildings and roads and killing 63 people.

HELPING HAND

The International Red Cross helps people during times of crisis. In 1906 the Red Cross provided medical aid and food for San Franciscans. Today, the Red Cross helps 30 million people each year when earthquakes or other natural disasters strike.

Kanto, Japan: 1923

Japan, like California, has been the site of many powerful earthquakes. An earthquake hit a Japanese region called Kanto less than 20 years after the San Francisco earthquake.

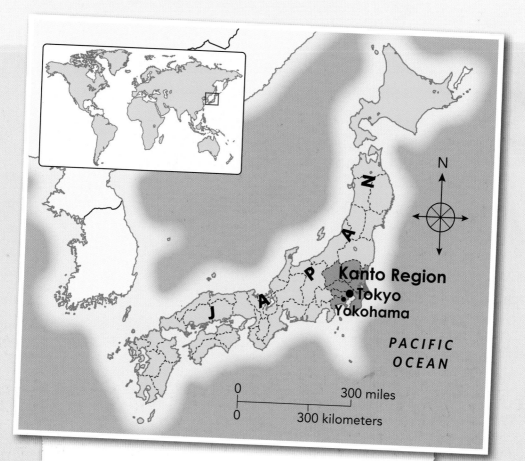

The Kanto region of Japan includes the country's capital and largest city, Tokyo.

DAILY LIFE

In 1923 a typical Japanese house would have been built out of wood, with a door made of rice paper.

Shigeo's story

Shigeo Tsuchiya lived in Yokohama, a city in the Kanto region (see map). As afternoon neared on September 1, 1923, Shigeo dashed home from school, eager for his lunch. At the table, he put a bowl of soup to his lips—and felt the earth move all around him. One of the world's deadliest earthquakes was beginning.

"Children, get out of the house," Shigeo's grandmother commanded. Shigeo started running. The earth continued to shake, throwing him to the ground three times. Each time, he got up and kept moving. His family sought safety on the edge of town. Along the way, Shigeo saw dead bodies lying underneath flattened buildings.

Tokyo was a large, bustling city in the years before the Kanto earthquake.

Wave of water

Near the coast, residents of the Kanto region faced another danger. The earthquake had stirred up a giant **tsunami**. Waves up to 12 meters (40 feet) high crashed onto the shore, destroying everything in their path. Shigeo's family escaped that horror. But they saw something just as bad.

The worst hours

As Shigeo ran, he heard someone shout, "Fire is coming." Across Yokohama, the earthquake had turned over the small **charcoal** stoves that most families used to cook their food. The homes, made out of wood and rice paper, quickly caught fire. The sky darkened with thick, black smoke.

After the earthquake, survivors began to clear away the **rubble** that filled the streets.

Hope from the ashes

The fires burned for almost two days. Many people died, and lots of buildings burned down. When Shigeo returned home, his house was nothing but ash. He later said, "I could smell it all day, a terrible smell."

Shigeo and his family used burned boards to build a simple shelter. Soon, food and supplies came from the government. Shigeo later recalled, "We began to build our house again, in exactly the same spot." He survived the great Kanto earthquake, though thousands more were not as lucky.

The Azume Bridge was destroyed by the earthquake (top), but by 1927 it had been rebuilt (bottom).

NUMBER CRUNCHING

This chart shows the destruction caused by the Kanto earthquake:

Number of people killed	around 142,800
Number of people injured	around 52,000
Number of people made homeless	around 3.25 million
Percentage of buildings destroyed in Tokyo	71 %
Percentage of buildings destroyed in Yokohama	86 %
Approximate value of losses (in today's dollars)	15.1 billion

Tangshan, China: 1976

Japan is not the only part of Asia often hit by deadly earthquakes. China has also seen its share of natural disasters, such as the one that struck Tangshan in 1976.

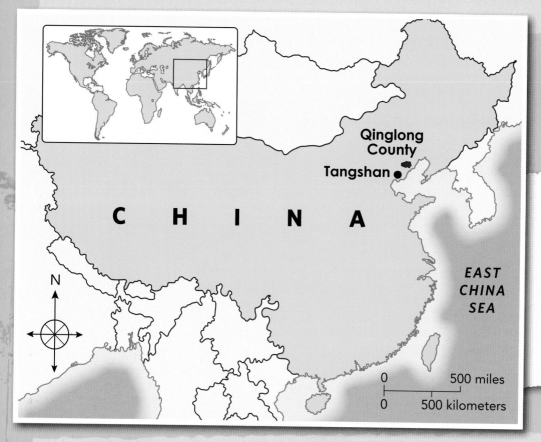

Qinglong County

Tangshan

C H I N A

EAST CHINA SEA

N

0   500 miles
0   500 kilometers

Tangshan and Qinglong County were both shaken by the huge earthquake of 1976.

Watching for disaster

Scientists in China were worried. Their studies warned that a major earthquake could strike during the summer of 1976. In Qinglong County, local officials took the warnings seriously. They told students to monitor equipment that showed if an earthquake was about to hit. Houses were likely to collapse if an earthquake struck, so thousands of tents were set up in preparation.

Caught off guard

In Tangshan, however, officials did nothing to prepare for possible disaster. When the earth began to tremble on July 28, seven-year-old Lan Shaoming and the other million city dwellers had no idea how difficult their lives were about to become.

Tangshan's Chengli Bridge was one of many bridges damaged or destroyed by the 1976 earthquake.

On the scene

Chinese officials said several strange things occurred before the Tangshan earthquake: "At 3:42 a.m., the sky over Tangshan lit up 'like daylight,' waking thousands who thought their room lights had been turned on. . . . Leaves on many nearby trees were burned to a crisp."

A survivor

For about 20 seconds, the ground shook beneath Tangshan. Thousands of buildings collapsed, killing people inside. "I just remember how frightened I was," Lan Shaoming said years later. He was lucky to survive. The Tangshan earthquake was one of the deadliest ever, with about 240,000 people killed.

Wang Ailing (left) was pulled from the rubble after the Tangshan earthquake. When another earthquake struck China in 2008, she went to the disaster area and gave money to help survivors.

Rebuilding Tangshan

Over several days, survivors tried to dig through the **rubble**, hoping friends and relatives were still alive. Meanwhile, the smell of dead bodies filled the air. The government did not have enough money to rebuild Tangshan quickly. It took more than 10 years. Today, Tangshan is once again a lively city. New buildings are designed so that they are not damaged by earthquakes. Still, Lao Shaoming and the other survivors will never forget the day their city was destroyed.

This memorial wall lists the names of some of the people killed in the 1976 earthquake. Visitors today leave flowers in their memory.

HELPING HAND

When another massive earthquake hit China in 2008, Lan Shaoming remembered how he had gone hungry as a child in 1976. "I can understand how people there must be feeling," he said. Like Wang Ailing, Lan used his own money to buy three truckloads of food and water to give to the victims of the earthquake.

Port-au-Prince, Haiti: 2010

The rebuilding of Tangshan offers hope to other cities struck by earthquakes. But in Haiti, hope was hard to find after a fierce earthquake struck in 2010.

Poverty and bad luck

Haiti is one of the poorest countries in the world. For many years, Haitians had flocked to Port-au-Prince seeking work. The newcomers crowded into small concrete houses that were poorly built. Most people did not have enough money to build a better house. The buildings were also not designed with earthquakes in mind, since they rarely happen in Haiti. When the earthquake struck, many buildings collapsed.

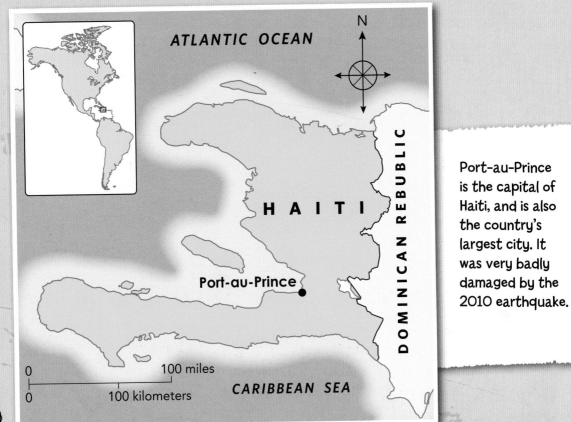

Port-au-Prince is the capital of Haiti, and is also the country's largest city. It was very badly damaged by the 2010 earthquake.

Darlene's story

Sixteen-year-old Darlene Etienne was sitting in her cousin's house when she and the rest of the people in Port-au-Prince felt the earth shake. The walls of the house crumbled, trapping Darlene under the **rubble**. Many other houses across the city and in nearby towns also crumbled.

Many Haitians struggled to survive after the severe damage caused by the earthquake.

DAILY LIFE

Across Haiti, almost 75 percent of the people live on less than two dollars per day. Hundreds of thousands of children do not go to school. Instead, they are forced to work as servants. They are not paid. They do the work just to make sure they have food and somewhere to live.

The search for survivors

The Haiti earthquake killed up to 230,000 people. Another million people were left homeless. For days, rescue workers searched for any clues that people might be alive in the rubble. As time went on, the chance of finding survivors fell. People died of their injuries if they did not receive medical treatment. Others died from a lack of water.

Here, rescue workers from Spain and Ireland, together with their search dog, look for survivors in Port-au-Prince.

HELPING HAND

Specially trained dogs helped some of the rescue teams. The dogs find the smell of a living person buried under rocks or concrete. They are trained to ignore all other smells. The dogs can also move easily through the rubble and work for 12 hours a day.

"A miracle"

Darlene Etienne was one of the lucky ones. The collapsed building did not completely crush her. She had space to lie down under the rubble. She also found some liquid to drink. Finally, after 15 days and close to death, Darlene's shouts for help were answered. She cried tears of joy as a team of French rescue workers pulled her out of the ruined building. One of the workers said, "I don't know how she happened to resist that long. It's a miracle."

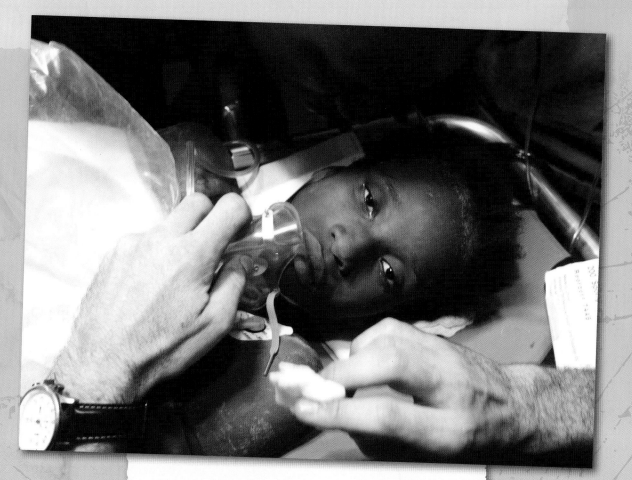

Darlene Etienne received medical treatment after her amazing battle for survival in the rubble of her cousin's house.

Medical aid

The rescue workers dug away at the rubble, so Darlene could breathe fresh air. After giving her some water, workers carefully pulled Darlene out of the rubble. Her leg was broken and she was weak, so she was rushed to a hospital. "I don't think she could have survived even a few more hours," a rescuer said. Doctors were amazed to see how quickly Darlene recovered. She soon ate her first food in days—mashed vegetables and yogurt.

Junior Alexis and Nadine Devilme were overjoyed to be reunited with their baby, who was lost during the Haiti earthquake.

HELPING HAND

Junior Alexis and Nadine Devilme spent days looking for their baby girl in the rubble of Port–au–Prince. A neighbor told them a baby had been rescued from their home. The parents then worked with the Red Cross and other international groups to find the baby, who was receiving medical care in Florida. The family was reunited in April 2010.

Helping the others

Before Darlene was rescued, food and supplies from around the world had reached Haiti. Tents were turned into homes and classrooms. The United States sent 22,000 soldiers to help give out supplies and provide medical care. Despite the massive relief effort, Haiti will need much more time and money to recover fully from the 2010 earthquake.

The U.S. Army brought clean water to hand out to survivors of the Haiti earthquake.

Conclusion

The study of earthquakes is called seismology. Some scientists study rocks along **faults** to see the signs of past earthquakes. The signs suggest that earthquakes can occur regularly—perhaps every 100 years. However, the scientists never know exactly when the next one will happen.

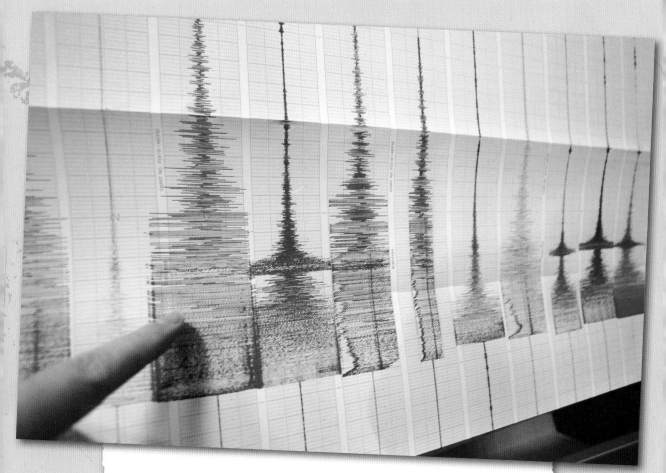

A seismograph records the **magnitude** of an earthquake. The blue lines here show activity from an earthquake that hit Taiwan in March 2010.

Preparing for the worst

In areas where earthquakes are common, people construct stronger buildings so that they will be more likely to survive. One way to make buildings stronger is to add extra steel beams. Unfortunately, these building methods are expensive, so they are rarely used in poorer countries.

Sometimes earthquakes are so powerful that they even destroy strong buildings. In March 2011, a huge earthquake in Japan destroyed many buildings and caused a devastating **tsunami**. Even though Japan was well prepared, thousands of people died, and almost half a million lost their homes.

Without Japan's earthquake warning systems and specially designed buildings, many more people could have died. People cannot prevent earthquakes, but they can work to reduce their effects.

NUMBER CRUNCHING

Scientists use the **Richter scale** to measure an earthquake's magnitude. The higher the number, the stronger the earthquake. The earthquake that struck north-eastern Japan in 2011 was extremely strong. Here is its magnitude compared to the four other major earthquakes discussed in this book:

Place of earthquake	Magnitude
Kanto, Japan	7.9
San Francisco, California	about 7.8
Port-au-Prince, Haiti	7.0
Tangshan, China	7.5
Northeastern Japan	9.0

Mapping Earthquakes

Earthquakes tend to strike more often in some areas than in others. However, no one can predict exactly where or when an earthquake will happen next.

San Francisco

NORTH AMERICA

ATLANTIC OCEAN

Port-au-Prince

PACIFIC OCEAN

SOUTH AMERICA

San Francisco, California

When this earthquake struck in 1906, it sparked fires that burned for almost three days, forcing several hundred thousand people to flee their homes. Many returned to find the buildings destroyed.

Port-au-Prince, Haiti

Crowded, poorly made houses and buildings collapsed quickly when an earthquake hit the Haitian capital of Port-au-Prince in 2010. The rebuilding there will cost several billion dollars.

Key

- Very high hazard
- High to moderate hazard
- Moderate hazard
- Low hazard
- Very low hazard

Kanto, Japan

Japan's Kanto region is the country's population and industrial center. The earthquake that hit in 1923 was the country's worst ever.

EUROPE

ASIA
Tangshan

Kanto

PACIFIC OCEAN

AFRICA

INDIAN OCEAN

AUSTRALIA

Tangshan, China

About 240,000 people died in 1976 when an earthquake struck Tangshan. Because of poor communications, the Chinese government did not learn about the disaster for 12 hours.

ANTARCTICA

Glossary

charcoal fuel made from wood that is often used for cooking

fault huge crack in the ground that can occur where tectonic plates meet

landslide when large amounts of earth and rocks slide down a mountain or hillside

magnitude power or strength of something

natural gas gas that is found naturally in the earth

refugee person forced out of his or her home because of a war or a natural disaster

Richter scale scale used to measure the destructive power of an earthquake

rubble broken pieces of rock or concrete created when a building is destroyed

tectonic plates giant, slow-moving slabs that make up Earth's surface

tremor strong shaking

tsunami giant, powerful ocean wave caused by an earthquake

Find Out More

Books

Jennings, Terry. *Earthquakes and Tsunamis* (*Amazing Planet Earth*). Mankato, Minn.: Smart Apple Media, 2010.

Spilsbury, Louise, and Richard Spilsbury. *Shattering Earthquakes* (*Awesome Forces of Nature*). Chicago: Heinemann Library, 2010.

Tagliaferro, Linda. *How Does an Earthquake Become a Tsunami?* (*How Does It Happen?*). Chicago: Raintree, 2010.

Van Rose, Susanna. *Volcanoes and Earthquakes* (*Eyewitness*). New York: Dorling Kindersley, 2008.

Websites

http://earthquake.usgs.gov/learn/kids/
This U.S. Geological Survey website contains lots of information for kids about earthquakes, including animations, puzzles, and games.

www.fema.gov/kids/quake.htm
This U.S. government website tells what to do in the event of an earthquake.

www.redcross.org/haiti
Visit this website to learn how the Red Cross is helping the victims of the earthquake in Haiti.

www.searchdogfoundation.org/98/html/index.html
This website is about the use of dogs as rescuers in natural disasters.

Index